IMAGES OF LONDON

HAMMERSMITH AND FULHAM PUBS

IMAGES OF LONDON

HAMMERSMITH
AND FULHAM PUBS

CHRIS AMIES

TEMPUS

Frontispiece: The Prince of Wales, 14 Lillie Road, in around 1910. Note the lavish inscription advertising 'Foreign Wines' on the frontage. The Prince of Wales is near to the Earl's Court exhibition halls and has a lot of seasonal traffic. It was rebuilt in the 1930s on the same ground plan.

First published 2004

Tempus Publishing Limited
The Mill, Brimscombe Port,
Stroud, Gloucestershire, GL5 2QG
www.tempus-publishing.com

British Library Cataloguing in Publication Data.
A catalogue record for this book is available from the British Library.

ISBN 0 7524 3253 2

Typesetting and origination by Tempus Publishing Limited.
Printed in Great Britain.

Contents

Acknowledgements

First of all I am immensely grateful to Jane Kimber, Anne Wheeldon and Francis Serjeant of the Hammersmith and Fulham Archives and Local History Centre for access to their photographic collection and for the great amount of help they afforded me. The value of their work in preserving the history – and by it the identity – of the borough cannot be overstated. The pictures in this book are sourced from the Archives' extensive collection held at:

The Archives and Local History Centre
Lilla Huset
191 Talgarth Road
London
W6 8BJ

Thanks also go to: The Fulham and Hammersmith Historical Society, in particular Keith Whitehouse for his help and suggestions with the text; Angela Dixon of the Hammersmith and Fulham Historic Buildings Group; Maya Donelan for her list of Fulham pubs; Jane Jephcote of the London Pubs Group; the landlords, managers and staff of several pubs in the London Borough of Hammersmith and Fulham; the *Fulham Chronicle*; and Alan R. Paterson, for copyright permission.

I have attempted to contact the owners of other photographs used in the book where the copyright owner has not been immediately traceable.

Introduction

The history of public houses in any town is linked with the history of the town itself, with progress towards industrialisation and urbanisation, and with changing demographic and social patterns.

In the London Borough of Hammersmith and Fulham these changes have often come rapidly. From being a riverside borough subsisting predominantly on market gardening, this area was built up suddenly in the late nineteenth century when the railways brought quicker commuting times into central London and thus increased the distances the urban middle classes were prepared to travel to work. A great number of the buildings in the borough have date plaques from the 1880s and 1890s; much of the housing stock, especially in Fulham and Brook Green, comprises terraces built by speculative constructors in the closing years of Queen Victoria's reign, with decoration ordered from a pattern book.

This burgeoning population needed feeding and watering. As a result, small local alehouses were demolished and rebuilt, most significantly in an upsurge of pub building in the 1890s. This occurred when the breweries started operating licensed houses directly rather than selling beer to independent publicans, and began redeveloping their pubs to attract more custom.

In 1890 the pubs of Fulham were audited by the Fulham Union Assessment Committee, who found seventy-eight for which names are given. Others may have been small, transient places or off-licences, though some, such as 180 North End Road – now the Old Oak – and 575 King's Road – later the Adelaide – have persisted as pubs. Sixty of this list are still in existence at the same address, though redevelopment has sometimes meant that a new pub will occupy a similar place to an old, even with a different address. The pubs of the older parts of Fulham – Fulham High Street and Walham Green, the area around Fulham Broadway – such as the King's Arms (Fulham Broadway) and the Golden Lion (Fulham High Street) have mostly survived in one form or another, and North End Road still has its pubs originally built to serve the market gardens and later the workers and customers of the local street market. Fulham has undergone less development in the twentieth century than Hammersmith, with the exception of housing estates built in North Fulham and along Lillie Road; its street plan and its fabric are still largely as they were 100 years ago.

Of a list of public houses in Hammersmith in 1722 which listed twenty-eight houses, eight still exist today. Others, such as the Rose and Crown (Hammersmith Road) and the Royal Oak (Glenthorne Road), kept going through the upheavals of Victorian urbanisation and have been lost more recently.

Hammersmith Borough Council's Law and Parliamentary Committee List in 1906 returned the names of 100 pubs in the Borough of Hammersmith. These include several around the Latimer Road area which is now covered by the Royal Borough of Kensington and Chelsea. Only fifty-two of the 100 houses listed survive. The whole of Hammersmith's town centre has changed with the construction of the A4 Great West Road and its flyover, as well as large-scale housing along and around Queen Caroline Street, the reconstruction of much of King Street and the Broadway and the demolition of the dense urban fabric – including five pubs – from the south side of Hammersmith Road to Great Church Lane. Fortunately, the riverside area, with its five pubs between Hammersmith Bridge and Chiswick, has been largely unaffected.

The northern part of the borough has pubs clustered along the Uxbridge Road, which was the main artery out of London in the days of coaching, and this was reflected in pub names such as the Telegraph and the Mail Coach (both now lost to redevelopment). Many of the public houses along this road and the Goldhawk Road which runs to the south of it cater for the large Irish community whose ancestors arrived in the nineteenth century and which has been involved particularly in the construction industry ever since. These houses, such as the Coningham Arms and the Shepherd and Flock, are not to be confused with the Irish-themed pubs that have become popular in recent years.

Through several decades of the twentieth century the pub was also an important place for live music. During the 1970s the Clarendon, the Red Cow, the Nashville Rooms, the Greyhound, the Swan at Fulham Broadway and the King's Head at Fulham High Street were leading venues. A decade or two later many pubs had rock or jazz acts, especially on a Sunday. Since 1989 this has all but vanished due to new laws requiring a music licence for more than two performers and the rise of satellite televisions showing sport.

By the 1980s a majority of pubs in England were owned by a handful of large industrial breweries. In 1989 the Monopolies and Mergers Commission found that the brewery combines were operating a monopoly and recommended that they be limited to owning a certain number of pubs, with the rest being sold off. In theory this should have given rise to a flowering of small local public houses, but in reality, although some did go into private hands, many pubs – especially in town centres – were bought up by PubCos, who often imposed a theme and a whimsical name or stripped out historic interiors to provide a single bland, more capacious and easily controlled interior space.

More positive trends are the rise of the pub as an eating place and the resurgence of real ale. In the decades after the Second World War the best food you could expect from most pubs was a cheese sandwich and a pork pie. Since the mid-1980s, public house food has been massively improved. The best pubs have added a good repertoire of food to a variety of beers and a comfortable and friendly atmosphere. The influence of the Campaign for Real Ale has helped in the reappearance of a variety of good ales and the preservation of notable pub interiors.

In 2003 there were 144 public houses in the borough, though the definition nowadays is sometimes hazy. The difference between a bar, a bar/restaurant and a pub is not always obvious. These houses, however, and those which have called Last Orders for the last time, form an integral part of our borough's history.

This book is their story.

one

The Early Days

The Barley Mow, around 1871. This was situated to the north of Brook Green at a time when that side of the Green was mostly orchards. The sign above the door reads 'Elizabeth Trowbridge'. Female licensees were not uncommon even in the nineteenth century. By 1894 the Barley Mow and the rural buildings nearby it had vanished, replaced by the speculative housing of what was known as 'West Kensington Park', which was neither a park nor in Kensington. The location of the Barley Mow would be somewhere around the present-day Sterndale Road.

The old King's Head in Fulham High Street. The King's Head is first mentioned in 1693 and is shown here in 1876. A replacement was built in 1884 but the house was knocked down in 1904 to make way for a tramway. The owners, who were well compensated, built a new, larger replacement pub.

The Bell and Anchor, which stood on the north side of Hammersmith Road next to Olympia until it was demolished in the late 1970s to make way for the Olympia lorry park. It was used for many years by magistrates for petty sessions and, according to Faulkner's history, had tasteful gardens with 'a good bowling green and a well-proportioned billiard room. During the early part of the reign of George III this house was much frequented by the nobility and gentry.' In February 1946 it hosted a touring exhibition of paintings of 'Londoners' England', including one of the Lyric, Hammersmith, by Ruskin Spear ARA.

The Red Lion at 490 Fulham Road was founded in the 1770s and enlarged and embellished, including the addition of a big stone lion on the roof, in the 1890s. The names of Watneys and Bass, which were to become famous later, are already prominent on this house.

Above: The Wheatsheaf, Fulham Road. The old Wheatsheaf was supposedly haunted by the ghost of its first landlord, Keene, who would be seen riding a donkey in the alleyway next to the pub. A stone discovered during demolition in 1889 bore the inscription KEEN 1616, bearing out the name of that landlord and the foundation date of the pub. In 1757 it was leased by the Bishop of London to James Sayers; the original house was pulled down in 1889 and rebuilt.

Left: The White Hart in Fulham Road at Fulham Broadway is first mentioned in the Churchwardens' accounts for 1632 and was originally known as the Beggar's Rest. This picture from 1885 also shows the offices of Gibbs and Flew, speculative builders, who were responsible for much of the 1870s and 1880s housing in the borough. The offices and the other small buildings there were demolished for the Fulham Town Hall extension in 1934, while the White Hart survives relatively unchanged.

The Eight Bells, 89 Fulham High Street, in 1880. Its name commemorates the upgrading of the peal of Fulham Church from six bells to eight in 1729. Previously in the area there was a pub called the Bell, which may be the same house. It was on the road to the river crossing until the old Fulham Bridge was replaced by Putney Bridge, further west, in 1886, and the resulting realignment of the bridge approach left the pub in a side street. The landlord of the Eight Bells complained of loss of income and was awarded £1,000. In the picture, which shows a very ornate Eight Bells frontage, note the greengrocer's apostrophe on the lamps: 'The Eight Bell's'.

Above: An etching in reverse by Theodore Roussell of the Duke's Head, 235 New King's Road, (now the Duke of Cumberland) in the late nineteenth century. Its precursor was the Pond Head (from 1710), which became notorious for rowdy behaviour, including the deaths of four gardeners in a fight. It became the Duke's Head in 1802. At the time the row of houses beyond the pub extended as far as its back wall; the two nearest were pulled down later and an extension to the pub built in 1980.

Left: A pre-1883 drawing from the work of C.J. Feret, the historian of Fulham, illustrating the now-lost Anchor In Hope pub in North End Road.

A token issued by the King's Arms, New King's Road, in 1656. Tokens were issued because of a shortage of coinage; the smallest coin in circulation was a penny, which would buy a considerable amount of beer, so smaller denominations had to be produced locally. The King's Arms was an alehouse in Henry VIII's time and became a coaching inn and staging post on the London to Southampton road, used by naval men on their way to the fleet.

The King's Arms, 425 New King's Road, in an illustration from 1878. It has been almost continuously in use since the time of Henry VIII, and was a coaching inn on the London to Southampton road. The house depicted was demolished and a replacement built in 1881.

Until the mid-nineteenth century the land each side of Uxbridge Road, a major thoroughfare westwards, was used for market gardens. The railway that is now the Hammersmith and City Line opened its station here in 1869, and trams began operation in 1874. By 1879 more than 128 acres of the borough's area had been taken for railways, and this led to an upsurge in building, especially on the rich land south of Uxbridge Road. New buildings included the Coningham Arms, 191 Uxbridge Road, built in 1881.

The Brewery Tavern, on the corner of Goldhawk Road and Shepherds Bush Green, some time in the nineteenth century. The tavern was on the site of a cottage once occupied by Miles Syndercombe, who plotted to assassinate Oliver Cromwell as he passed by there in January 1657. There were several small breweries in the borough in the nineteenth century, most of which vanished during the amalgamations of the twentieth century.

A coach trip outside the Crown and Sceptre, Melina Road, Shepherds Bush, in the late nineteenth century. The Crown and Sceptre is still going, externally similar to the picture, and popular with Queen's Park Rangers supporters.

The old Queen Adelaide on Uxbridge Road, some locals, and a collection of horse-drawn vehicles. Named after the consort of William IV and probably built some time in the 1840s, this pub was rebuilt with its distinctive turret in 1895. This is a listed building.

Above: The Black Lion, South Black Lion Lane, near the Thames. This is now a listed building and is seen here in the 1880s with the tower of St Peter's Church (Edward Lapidge, 1829) visible to the left. The Black Lion achieved fame or infamy in 1804 when an excise officer, Francis Smith, shot a white-clad bricklayer, Francis Millwood, whom he had mistaken for the 'Hammersmith Ghost', which was said to haunt the churchyard and leap out at passers-by. Millwood's body was taken to the nearby Black Lion and an inquest held there. At the Old Bailey, Smith was sentenced to death, but received a royal pardon and his sentence commuted to a year's imprisonment.

Above: An early riverside pub, the Swan was built in the late seventeenth century at a ferry crossing just east of where Putney Bridge now stands, and had tea gardens leading down to the Thames. On the night of 18 September 1871 the Swan burned down and was never rebuilt. A malthouse behind the pub survived until at least 1894 but had been demolished by 1913, when the area was still known as 'Swan Wharf'. The name has since disappeared from the map. There are now no riverside pubs on the north bank between the Crabtree (p.27) and Chelsea.

Opposite below: The Duke of Sussex, on the corner of Sussex Place and (Hammersmith) Bridge Road, around 1870, with regulars posing for their picture. This pub, along with Sussex House (once the home of Captain Marryat) was probably named after HRH Augustus Frederick, Duke of Sussex's association with the area. This fine, simple building is no more.

Above: The Hampshire Hog on King Street and a group of locals in a photograph from 1880. The painter Evacustes Phipson based a painting on this photograph. As the Hog, this pub appears in official records for 1722, and in 1741 the buildings and land comprised half an acre, but the current building is much more recent.

Left: The original Greyhound, on Greyhound Road opposite Margravine Road, was an eighteenth-century building replaced in the nineteenth century by a new house on the corner of Fulham Palace Road. This in turn was demolished in 1882 and replaced by the 'New Greyhound'. This picture shows the old Greyhound in around 1880.

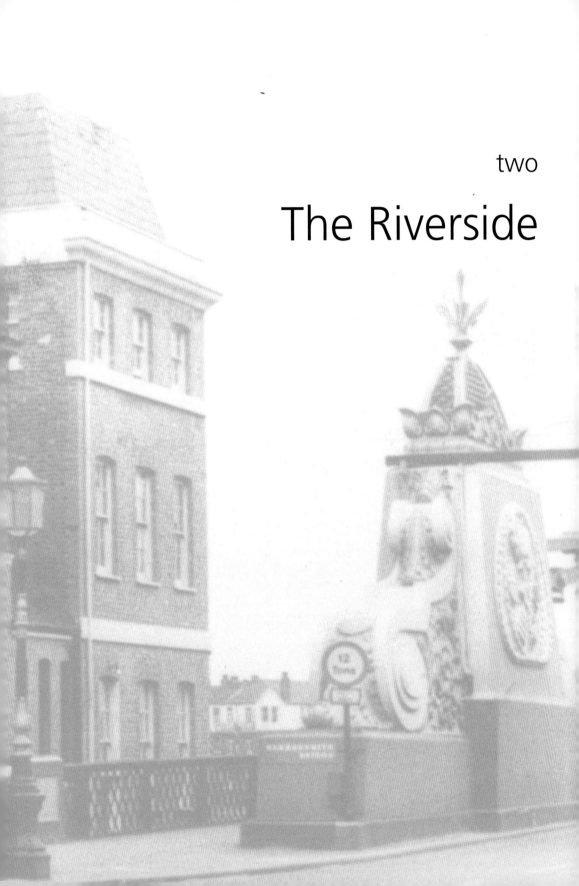

two

The Riverside

The Black Lion and a traction engine in a postcard from 1936. The novelist Sir Alan ('A.P.')
Herbert was a regular at the Black Lion during the 1950s and wrote a letter to the *Morning Post*
defending the pub from the Liquor Commission, who wanted it closed down as 'redundant'.

A skittle match at the Black Lion on 8 June 1928. The skittle alley has vanished to be replaced by
a patio garden at the front of the pub, and the piggery that previously abutted the pub has also
disappeared. A.P. Herbert, who was president of the skittle club, is seventh from left in the back
row of spectators.

Two of the Thames-side pubs – the Rutland and, beyond it, the Blue Anchor – shown on 2 August 1974. The Blue Anchor is the older house, appearing on the 1722 Victuallers' List. Gustav Holst composed his *Hammersmith Suite* in the pub's upper rooms. The Rutland dates from the 1880s and lost its top floor and viewing platform during the Second World War.

The Old City Arms is at the foot of Hammersmith Bridge Road, just by the bridge. It was originally opened some time between 1812 and 1828 but was burnt down in 1847 and rebuilt. A newspaper column from 1839 says 'We advise that old fool Hetherington, of the City Arms, to stay at home instead of going out shooting, leaving his interesting wife by herself.' In 1973-74 the Old City Arms was called the Harlequin and laboured under a garish colour scheme, but sanity has prevailed since.

Above: This seventeenth-century portico is all that remains of the original Ship Inn, and is now Grade II listed. The Ship on Upper Mall (renamed the Old Ship to distinguish it from the newer Ship on the corner of Ship Lane and Bridge Road) is one of the oldest pubs in Hammersmith, though the present building is slightly west of the seventeenth-century original.

Left: The Old Ship in the pre–First World War period. Engineers at Thorneycrofts gathered there in 1897 to plan a strike calling for an eight-hour day. In 1914 it narrowly escaped closure as 'redundant'. Originally, the Old Ship, a pub among Hammersmith's former riverside industries, faced away from the river, but in 1974 it was remodelled so that the main entrance faced the Thames. This pub has a long and locally significant history.

Above: Men playing bumblepuppy (the old game of nineholes) in the Dove, around 1930. On the right is George Burnham (1855-1936). Built in the eighteenth century – it is mentioned in a valuation from 1793 – the Dove was originally a coffee house and was purchased by Fuller Smith and Turner in 1796. Its name has alternated over the years between the 'Dove' and the 'Doves', possibly because it was originally named after its owner, thus 'Dove's house'. This picture was provided by Alan R. Paterson, the great-great-grandson of George Burnham.

Right: The Dove, Upper Mall, looking towards Chiswick. The Dove's 'snug' is said to be the smallest pub bar in England, with just four stools and a plaque showing the high water mark in the 1928 flood. The main bar is divided by two flights of stairs, which lead to a conservatory (built in 1986) overhung with a vine. In *The Water Gipsies*, A.P. Herbert called it 'The Pigeons'.

The Doves, as seen from the river, with a collection of locals watching the swans, probably some time in the 1950s or 1960s. The pub is Grade II listed and is one of the most historic features of Hammersmith's waterfront.

The new Crabtree, built in the closing years of the nineteenth century, was a far bigger building than its precursor and had pretensions as a hotel. This picture dates from April 1962. The new Crabtree shares the same relationship with the river, being situated next to a beach overhung by a willow tree and passed by the Thames path, which goes inland briefly at this point. This is an historic area, the last of the old wharf districts with access to the river along the entirety of Hammersmith and Fulham's riverside.

A group of locals and a policeman outside the Old Crabtree in around 1895. This, like many other houses in the area at the time, belonged to Sich's Brewery of Chiswick. Notice also a sign for the Royal Humane Society on the wall.

The Old Crabtree, in Rainville Road by the Fulham Riverside, was originally the Three Jolly Gardeners, but was later given the name of Crabtree that had been applied to the area since medieval times. Founded in the 1760s, the house is shown here shortly before its demolition in 1898. It particularly served the local market gardens, hence the name, and was on the edge of the land of the last local farmers, the Matyear family. The last Matyear farmer, William, died in 1910.

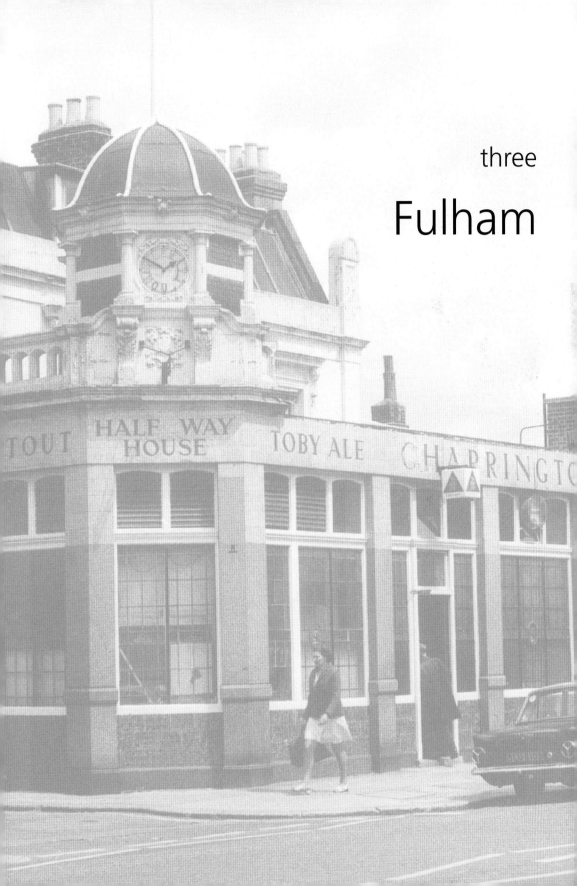

three

Fulham

Coronation celebrations at the Alma, Parsons Green Lane, in 1937. The Alma was built in 1899 on the site of an earlier house dating back to 1799. In the 1851 Post Office Directory, two beer retailers are shown in Parsons Green Lane, but neither house is named. The Alma would have been named after the Battle of the Alma (1854).

The Atlas, 16 Seagrave Road, pictured on 16 September 1974. This pub just off Lillie Road was built in 1868. It was damaged in the Second World War when a bomb hit the houses opposite, and the upper floor had to be rebuilt. Although the public and saloon bars have been knocked through into one, this has been done without obliterating the original character; in the last decade the pub has been restored to its Victorian style. There is a secluded garden to the side.

Earl Attlee, Clem Attlee's son, opening the Clem Attlee on the Lillie Road estate in April 1971. This picture first appeared in the *Fulham Chronicle* for 16 April 1971 and is used with permission.

The Clem Attlee, Rylston Road, Fulham, was opened in April 1971 as an estate pub for the Clem Attlee estate, replacing an older house called the Lord Clyde. For some reason it has recently been renamed the Pump House.

Left: The Wellington, Haldane Road, on 18 January 1974. This is a large Irish pub that sits in a suburban Fulham street next to a youth club.

Below: The Crown Hotel on Lillie Road, originally founded before 1771 on the junction of North End Road and what was then Crown Road. The present house was built in 1890 at a rateable value of £240 – one of the highest in the borough. Seen here in 1903 with a small group of curious onlookers, the 'Crown' name only appears at the top of the large sign, while the frontage advertises the name of the licensee, E.A. Cook. The Crown has since been known as the Fulham Volunteer (from December 1974), the Fulham Tap, the Goose and Granite, and now the Goose. The marbling on the pillars has been painted out white.

Opposite below: The Cock, 360 North End Road, first appears in 1713 and the present house was built in 1895. The Fulham Baths are visible to the left of the pub, behind the coach, in this picture taken in 1974.

Above: The Golden Gloves at 80 Fulham Palace Road was previously the Rifle, and under the tutelage of the Mancini family (note the sign: 'Alf & Tony Mancini') became a shrine to boxing, with pictures and memorabilia on the walls as well as a scarlet carpet with a golden gloves motif. The welterweight Tony Mancini lost only two of his seventy-two fights as a professional between 1950 and 1962. The Gloves also hosted live music on most nights of the week during the 1980s. It is pictured here on 24 January 1974. In the mid 1990s, the Mancinis sold the pub, whereupon it became the Old Suffolk Punch and is now a modern bar called by an abbreviation of that name, 'OSP'.

A QUARTET OF CHAMPIONS.

E. T. PIMM'S
"Sam Lavender."   A. Shrubb.   G. A. Olley.   Tommy Burns
(*Bull Terriers.*)   (*Running.*)   (*Cycling.*)   (*Boxing.*)

E. T. PIMM.   THE COCK HOTEL, ::
WALHAM GREEN, S.W.

Left: E.T. Pimm, landlord of the Cock from 1903-15, portrayed with his champion dog Sam Lavender and three other champions on a card postmarked 5 November 1909.

Below: E.T. Pimm's celebrated bull terriers and their handler, some time before the First World War.

Opposite below: Building the extension to the Duke of Cumberland on 26 September 1980.

E. T. PIMM'S CELEBRATED BULL TERRIERS:
"East Hill Daisy," Champion "Sam Lavender," "Bob Lavington" and "St. James Beauty."
"COCK HOTEL," WALHAM GREEN, LONDON, S.W.

The Duke of Cumberland, 19 February 1974, with a Young's brewer's dray outside. The present house is a baroque, three-storey building designed by R. Cruwys, built in 1892 and given its present name in May 1971. It has an elaborate traditional interior including a Fulham Potteries tiled wall (installed in the 1970s with tiles removed from elsewhere) and original paintings. The Duke of Cumberland is Grade II listed.

Pictured here on 4 March 1980 when it was a Charrington pub, the Adelaide at 575 King's Road was built in 1858 and in 1999 became an upmarket bar/restaurant called Lunasa. The single-storey rear extension in the picture has been redeveloped with a second storey and blended into the overall line of the building. The water tower in the picture has also vanished. The bar layout and the ornate windows have been preserved in its latest incarnation.

The George, 506 Fulham Road, on the corner of North End Road, in March 1962. The George is first referred to in the will of Sir William Powell, dated 2 December 1680. It was rebuilt in 1867 and was owned by Richard Hartley, who also ran a bus service and was a clerk at the Bank of England. The bank's governors told him he would either have to give up running bus services or lose his job at the bank. He gave up the bank as the buses paid better and he could work from home. Fulham's first police station was built in Lewis's Yard behind the George in 1830.

The Durell Arms, 704 Fulham Road, on the corner of Munster Road, was built in 1868 and is now known simply as the Durell following a period as the Rat and Parrot. It is depicted here on 24 January 1979.

The 'new' Wheatsheaf, seen in 1891 with a group of locals and probably the landlord (R. Bartholomew) and his wife by the main door, with their bar staff next to them. Curiously, the advertising on the outside of the pub speaks of wines and spirits, and not at all of beer. The curved gables have since vanished, possibly due to wartime damage, and the front of the house has been painted white with a black pattern instead of the thoughtful brickwork seen here. There is now also an extension to the left of the house which gives it the address 582 Fulham Road.

Above: A subdued Eight Bells, Fulham High Street, on a windy day in around 1962 when it was owned by Mann's. In 1978 the house was firebombed; it has since been extensively refurbished and is now a popular and family-friendly local. The carriage entrance to the right is still in existence, though the lamps by the entrance, which were in place in 1880 and 1962, are no longer there.

Above: The Glen, a combined Bass Charrington pub and off-licence at 137 Stephendale Road in the southern part of Fulham. Founded in 'AD 1959' it is seen here on 23 March 1973. This is now one of the two So Bars in the borough.

Right: The Harwood Arms, 29 Walham Grove, on 10 September 1974. Sited just east of Fulham Broadway (otherwise known as Walham Green), the current Italianate house was built in 1904, replacing a mid-nineteenth century pub.

Opposite below: The Golden Lion at 57 Fulham High Street was built in 1894, replacing a house constructed in 1836 on the site of a Tudor public house called the Anchor. A legend has grown up around this earlier house, claiming it to have been in the possession of the notorious 'burning bishop', Edmund Bonner, and also to have been frequented by William Shakespeare himself. The Anchor was later called the White House, and was renamed the 'Golden Lion' in 1787 by its owner Thomas Giddens. This picture was taken in the snow on 24 January 1979. To the right posters advertise acts such as Elvis Costello and Horslips.

The Halfway House, at 316 Lillie Road, on 1 July 1974. Note the off-licence to the right of the picture. Off sales were formerly important to pubs, giving patrons a chance to buy beer to take home. Probably because of the increasing dominance of supermarket sales this market has declined. The Halfway House was built on the front garden of an earlier nineteenth-century house. It used to possess a clock which only had six numbers: 12 and 5 in black, and 11, 1, 3 and 6 in red. These were the opening and closing times on weekdays and Sundays (in red) when it was made before 1914. The Halfway House is now called the Chancery; the off-licence to the right of the pub is now a shop. The Halfway House clock at the corner has sadly been removed.

The Lord Palmerston, 648 King's Road, was originally built in or around 1862 and rebuilt in 1895. Since the picture was taken on 11 July 1974, it has been known as the Babushka House and is now called the Morrison.

The Lillie Langtry, 19 Lillie Road, is named after the Jersey-born actress (1853-1929) who started out as a society belle and owed her stage career to having inadvertently offended the Prince of Wales. The Langtry began life as the Lillie Arms in the early twentieth century, and took its present name in April 1979. It is seen here on 13 February 1981. The pub on the other side of the road is the Prince of Wales (picture on page 2).

The Salisbury Tavern, 21 Sherbrooke Road, on 15 November 1976. Built in the late nineteenth century by the speculative builders Gibbs and Flew, the Salisbury was the centre of the Salisbury estate and one of the larger pubs on the assessment list of 1890, with a gross value of £240 which the local Council proposed to increase to £750, the largest rate in the borough. It is still in existence on the corner of Sherbrooke and Dawes Roads.

The Hand and Flower, 617 King's Road, on 11 August 1987. Founded some time before 1841, this house was rebuilt in 1897 as an opulent Victorian tavern for the King's Road traffic. It is now called Jim Thompson's.

The Jolly Brewer, 308–310 North End Road, some time around the start of the twentieth century, at the height of its decorative charm. Serving the North End Road market, it is still in use although has had a couple of name changes in recent years.

The Jolly Maltster, 17 Vanston Place, pictured in around 1912. The sign to the left shows the site of the Red Hall cinema, opened in December 1913 and now a bingo hall. The original Jolly Maltster was built in the seventeenth century and the current house dates from 1900. During the rebuilding, coins of the reign of Charles I and a mummified cat were found.

The Jolly Maltster on 17 November 1973 when it was a Courage house. The tiled signs advertising 'Royal Brewery Ales' have been restored since this picture was taken. The Jolly Maltster is popular with Chelsea FC supporters.

The King's Head, 490 Fulham Road, on 14 May 1981. The King's Head claims a foundation date of 1680. The present building, with its bay windows and stone plaque, dates from around 1880. It is currently known as the Slug and Lettuce.

The King's Head, Fulham Road, in around 1905. Walham Green Station, since renamed Fulham Broadway, can be seen on the right of the picture, with a very large sign advertising reduced fares to the City and Charing Cross.

The old Norman Arms, on the corner of Lillie Road and Rylston Road, with a number of locals enjoying a sunny day in 1910. This imposing building was unfortunately replaced by a rather uninspiring estate pub.

The new Norman Arms, one of the pubs for the Clem Attlee estate (the other is the Pump House), on 1 July 1974.

Above: The 'new' King's Arms, 425 New King's Road, on 6 February 1982. In the 1920s the saloon bar was allegedly the largest in London, with waiter service for drinks in the evenings. This largely lost practice is the profession of a leading character in *20,000 Streets under the Sky*, the 1935 novel by Patrick Hamilton. The pub was closed for some years in the 1990s before reopening in 2002 as the Larrik.

Left: Founded in 1773 and rebuilt in 1831, the Peterborough Arms at 65 New King's Road was renamed the Southern Cross in 1989. It was the birthplace of a benevolent society for poor relief founded in 1833 by John Butt and Samuel Walden to commemorate the passing of the Reform Bill; this became the Peterborough Benevolent Society and later met in the Red Lion at Walham Green.

Celebrations for the coronation of King George VI in 1937 at Walham Green, showing the Swan, 1 Fulham Broadway. The Swan was then a Barclay Perkins house and still in possession of its swan sculpture on the roof. The separate doors for the public and saloon bars are visible towards the right-hand end of the façade. The Swan, a major music venue for the area in the 1980s, is now an Irish-themed pub known as Brogan's.

The Weavers Arms, 18 Farm Lane, on 10 September 1974. Built in 1930, it is a short distance from the Jolly Maltster and, like that pub, is popular with supporters of Chelsea FC. In 1993 it was renamed the Fulham Dray. Someone has written EVERTON on the wall on the right-hand side of the picture: a bold or foolish move in such a Chelsea-dominated area.

Above: The Maltster, Vanston Place, four years before it was redeveloped as the Jolly Maltster in 1900. Signboards advertise 'Smith's Welsh Ales' and 'Mann Crossman and Paulin's'. There is a funeral parlour to the left. Observe the two men lounging against a lamp-post, the figure in the porch and the man in a cap to the left of the picture, who seems to be the victim of a double-exposure: the fence is visible through him.

Right: A business card from 1905 for the Queen Elizabeth, 58 Bagley's Lane. The lane, which is in the south-eastern part of Fulham, is named after the Bagley family, who owned market gardens in the area in the mid-nineteenth century. The Queen Elizabeth was in existence by 1890, when it appears in the list of local rated premises.

Below: The Queen Elizabeth in 1973. In 2001 there was a proposal to turn this site into homes, which would have deprived the area's residents of their one real local pub. The development plans were rejected by the Council after protest by ARISE (the Association of Residents In Sands End).

Opposite below: The Mitre started life as a small local pub and was rebuilt in 1895 on the junction of Dawes Road and Bishops Road in central Fulham. Depicted here on 11 July 1974, it had a makeover in 2003, the extent of which can be seen by comparing the house as it is now with the pictures that are on display inside.

THE "QUEEN ELIZABETH,"
58, Bagley's Lane,
Fulham, S.W.

Proprietor   ·   ·   ·   FRANK ADAMS.

The Nell Gwynne at 541 King's Road, just over the bridge from Chelsea, is an old pub, probably rebuilt in the late nineteenth century during the speculative pub building of those years. Currently known as One and formerly as Scruffy Murphy's and Come the Revolution, it was used in the Hylda Baker television series *Not on your Nellie* as the Brown Cow. It is seen here on 7 November 1978, when it was a Watneys pub.

The Wilton Arms, 203-5 Dawes Road, on 11 July 1974. A small local pub in the nineteenth century, it was rebuilt in 1893 and remodelled in the 1930s with a third storey.

The Old Rose in Sands End Lane, in 1895. The earliest notice of the Rose occurs in the minutes of a Court General in 1708, when it was transferred from Francis Whettman to Richard Sanders to use as an inn. Shooting competitions were common there in the early nineteenth century. This row of houses, including the Old Rose, was demolished when the Imperial Gas Company extended its gasworks in the early twentieth century.

Shown on 9 December 1972, the Rose at 1 Harwood Terrace near the Imperial gasworks is now called the Legless Tup. It replaced the Old Rose (q.v.) though both were in operation at the same time in the late nineteenth century.

Above: The Rising Sun, 477 Fulham Road, was first licensed in 1855 to John Newton. It is directly opposite Chelsea FC's Stamford Bridge ground, and has variously been called the Stamford Bridge Arms, Stamfords, the Cross Eyed Newt, and most recently the Greene Room. It is shown here on 7 November 1978 during the construction of traffic-calming measures at the entrance to Holmead Road, a former rat run between Fulham Road and King's Road.

Right: The Cottage, formerly the Cottage of Content, at 21 Colehill Lane, a residential street to the east of Fulham Palace Road. Depicted here on 3 May 1975 when it was a Watneys house, the Cottage was built in 1886.

Below: In 1968, when this picture was taken, the late nineteenth-century Princess Royal was a Watneys pub on the corner of Waterford Road and Moore Park Road. It is now a modern gastro-bar called the Pelican. Note the policeman helping an elderly lady across the road in the foreground of the picture!

Opposite below: The White Horse, 1-3 Parsons Green, was established in 1688 and first mentioned in Parish Books in 1777. The present house was built in 1886 and is seen here in 1962 when it was a free house owned by the James family. It has since become renowned for its wide range of ales; beer writer Michael Jackson rates it as one of three classic pubs in London along with the Dove at Hammersmith and the White Cross at Richmond.

The Britannia, on the corner of Britannia Road and Fulham Road, on 7 November 1978. A large sign advertises 'Live Family Entertainment, Star Cabarets, Good Food'. This house is now called the So Bar.

THE ALMA TAVERN

Opposite Parsons Green Tube
Tel: 01 - 736 4596

BRING THIS LEAFLET and you get
2 DRINKS for the price of one.

MONDAY *** CD Juke Box on FREE Play

THURSDAY *** TOM PUGH KARAOKE SINGALONG

SUNDAY *** An evening of Irish Entertainment

Every Day & Night DOUBLES of Vodka,
Scotch, Rum & Gin Only £1.20

Function Room Available

Video Games

Pool Room

THE ALMA, PARSONS GREEN LANE LONDON SW6

Left: A leaflet from the Alma, 51 Parsons Green Lane, for August 1989, advertising 'CD Jukebox on Free Play, Karaoke, and Irish Entertainment'. In 1990 the Alma became a bar called Cramps and is now called the Pen.

Right: The Wandsworth Bridge Tavern, 360 Wandsworth Bridge Road, depicted in 1900 with a precarious load of boxes on a horse-drawn cart. The tavern advertises itself as the First and Last Pub in Fulham. It is currently known as the Goose, and has been known as the Bridge, Paddy's Goose, and the Pickled Newt.

Opposite below: The New Golden Lion (seen here on 19 November 1974) is one of several names borne by the former Red Lion at 490 Fulham Road. It became a nightclub in the 1980s and is now a Latin-American bar called Havana.

The current 'King's Head', 4 Fulham High Street, was built in 1905 and is shown here just after that date. The three-storey building on the right of it was a block of flats called King's Mansions, owned by the pub, and which was replaced by a beer garden in 1980 when it was found to be subsiding into Fulham Palace Moat. The King's Head itself is Grade II listed. It is externally largely unchanged and is now a popular rock music venue.

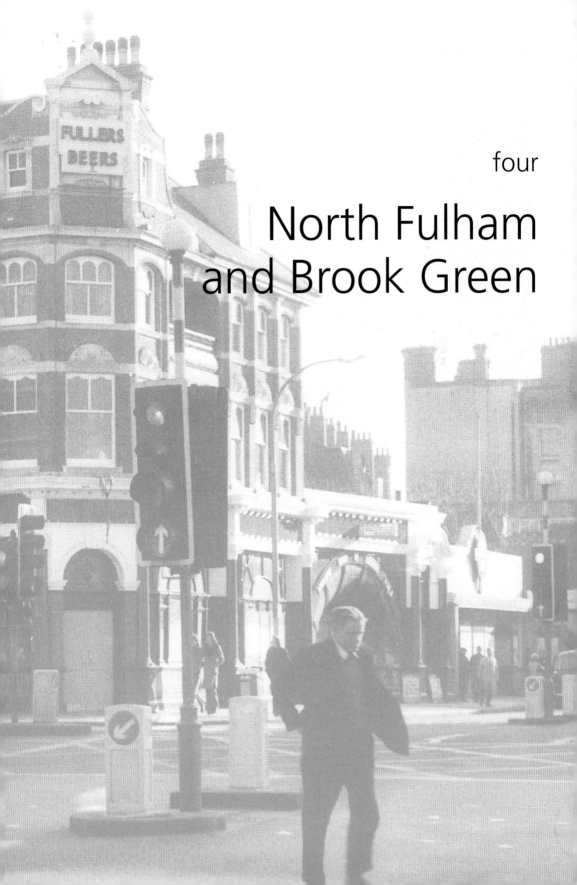

four

North Fulham
and Brook Green

Above: A charabanc party at the Greyhound, Fulham Palace Road, in the 1920s. From left to right, standing: Mr Bridges, – , William Earles, Mr Brown, Fred Hunt, – , Thomas Earles, – , – , Con? (fishmonger from Greyhound Road), Mr Bridges, – . Seated: 'Taffy' Earles, – . Greyhound Road, which leads from Fulham Palace Road eastwards here, contains two other pubs: the Colton Arms at no.187, built in 1858 by George Colston More and originally named the Colston Arms, and the Queen's Arms at no.171 – a small local pub built around 1880 and refitted in the 1960s. Another house, the Prince of Wales at no.147, was demolished in the twentieth century and the site is now occupied by housing.

Opposite above: The Hand and Flower, 1 Hammersmith Road, in the early twentieth century. In the 1890 assessment of Fulham public houses, the Hand and Flower has the highest rated value, at £250. The Hand and Flower was originally the Rose and Crown and was rebuilt some time after 1788 by William Vale, who gave it a new name referring to the nearby Vineyard Nursery.

Opposite below: The management and staff of the Hand and Flower, Hammersmith Road, in the 1950s. Left of picture is probably Jack Levy, the landlord. Levy was the landlord there from 1929 until his death, aged eighty-eight, in 1975.

The Cedars Hotel was built in 1883 by speculative builders Gibbs and Flew as the estate pub – but what an estate pub! – for the Cedars estate, a late nineteenth-century speculative build by Gibbs and Flew that occupies several streets between Hammersmith Road, the present A4, North End Road and the former St Paul's School off Gliddon Road. Here it is depicted around 1900, with an interesting selection of horse and handcarts in front.

When the North End Road was straightened – so that the original line of the road round the Cedars Hotel became North End Crescent – an architecturally rather unsatisfying wing was added to the Cedars to give it a frontage on the North End Road again. The new wing gives access to a music club which is currently called West One Four, was previously the Orange, and in this picture from 8 June 1973 is called the Bird's Nest. The 'Warming Pan' signs along the pub frontage refer to a bar within the Cedars. The pub itself is now known as the Fox, with various suffixes – previously Fox Rat and Carrot and currently Fox Rattle and Hum.

The Albion, 121 Hammersmith Road, in a picture from 14 February 1981. Part of a small retail and residential complex designed by Melville Seth-Ward in the Dorcas Conservation Area, it was built in 1923, first called the Albion Beerhouse and owned by the Camden Brewery. It is on the corner of Munden Street, at the other end of which – at 1 Vernon Street – was a pub called the Rising Sun. This was recorded in 1871 and again in 1910, but its site is now occupied by modern housing.

The Pear Tree, in Margravine Road, was originally built to serve the market gardens, as its name implies. Depicted here in 1977, it was built in 1878 and is on the local register of significant buildings for its well-preserved exterior including decorative ironwork over the entrances, a terracotta name plaque and lionhead panels, granite facing to the extension and a hanging sign.

Above: The Old Oak on North End Road started as a beerhouse and was rebuilt in the late nineteenth century and again in the 1930s.

Left: The Royal Oak, Milson Road, on 14 October 1972. Another small pub serving the people of the Brook Green area, this has now become a pub-restaurant called the Priory.

Opposite below: The 'new' Seven Stars is a streamlined 1930s building and an intact example of inter-war pub architecture. Since this picture was taken (in November 1969), the 'Fuller Smith and Turner' inscription has been replaced by a more conventional banner sign giving the pub's name.

Above: The 'old' Seven Stars, 253 North End Road, depicted in 1896. It was a local public house serving the market garden trade, and was mentioned in the parish books for 1771. It was assessed in 1890 at a gross value of £96: larger than nearby houses like the Bold Crispin, 25 Star Road (£40), but considerably smaller than the big inns such as the Cedars Hotel (£240).

Left: The Barons Court, 28 Comeragh Road, on 2 June 1973. Variously known as the Barons Court Tavern, in 1985 it became the Barons Alehouse. In the early 1990s it was renamed The Curtain's Up, referring to the Barons Court Theatre in the pub's vaulted cellar.

Below: The Elm, North End Road, was rebuilt in 1898 and has interesting architectural detailing on the cornice.

Opposite below: During the 1970s the former Three Kings on North End Road was a country music venue called the Nashville Rooms owned by the owners of the Red Cow on Hammersmith Road. Later this too became a rock venue, and bands would try out at the Red Cow and move on to the Nashville if they were successful there. By the end of the 1970s the Nashville Rooms was derelict, but it was reopened in the early 1980s as the Three Kings. It has generally remained open since, being renamed the Via Fossa in 1997 and the Famous Three Kings or F3K in 2000. It is shown here on 26 November 1973.

Above: The Three Kings at 171 North End Road dates back to the mid-seventeenth century but in its present form was built in 1904 as a railway pub to service the nearby Fulham North End station, which has since been renamed West Kensington (though it isn't in Kensington). It is an imposing building with a remarkable piece of curved glass over the entrance. The cottages to the left of the picture were demolished when the A4 was built in the 1950s.

Above: The Clarence, a small family pub at 148 North End Road, was founded in 1864 and enlarged in 1894. Here it is depicted while a Watneys pub on 24 January 1974 – it has not changed substantially since this time. The Clarence is currently owned by Conway Taverns who also own the Princess Victoria on Uxbridge Road.

Left: The Cumberland Arms, on the corner of North End Road and Cumberland Crescent, on 26 November 1973, a Whitbread pub with no visible sign of its name. Where the Cumberland Arms is now was 'a pretty country house known as Cumberland Lodge', dilapidated in Maclure's Survey of 1853 and pulled down shortly afterwards. Cumberland Crescent and the Arms were built in 1857. The Cumberland Arms soldiered on for many years as an Irish local pub, and in 2003 reopened with a remodelled interior and a wider selection of beers.

Opposite below: The Live and Let Live at 35-37 North End Road started out as one of the pubs, along with the nearby Cumberland Arms, catering for the market garden workers of North Fulham. Depicted here on 26 November 1973, it later became the Pickled Newt but now fortunately has reverted to its original name as a Greene King house, though less admirably the tiling on the lower walls has been painted over.

Above: The annual outing of the regulars from the Live and Let Live, in the 1914 season. Their smartness of dress (including straw boaters) seems to be in inverse proportion to their cheerfulness. The boys in the front row in particular look less than thrilled with the concept of an outing. The original of this picture was sent as a postcard and postmarked 28 August 1914.

A pensioners' charabanc party outside the Havelock, Irving Road/Milson Road, probably in the 1930s. The Havelock survives as one of several small pubs serving the area between Brook Green and Shepherd's Bush.

The Duke of Edinburgh, Woodstock Grove W12, on 9 April 1974. This small corner pub dates from the late nineteenth century, as does much of the housing in the area.

The Old Parr's Head, at 120 Blythe Road in Brook Green, in August 1981. The Parr's Ditch, now culverted, ran nearby along the western edge of Brook Green, but it is likely the name refers to a near-legendary, long-lived and notorious seventeenth-century character. Blythe Road was previously called 'Blind Lane' and according to Faulkner (1831) was 'sadly neglected and nearly impassable during the winter season'. The Old Parr's Head was built between 1871 and 1873, and in the street directory of 1898-99 is licensed to one with the remarkable name of Disney Perou.

The Greyhound, 175-177 Fulham Palace Road, on 21 October 1978. During the later decades of the twentieth century the Greyhound became, in the words of its manager Duncan Ferguson, 'a nationally-recognised centre for progressive music'. In 1971 neighbours raised a thirty-name petition against the 'noise' from the pub, but Paul Brett of the progressive group Sage raised 3,000 signatures in favour of the music. Bob Marley was among the artists to have played at the Greyhound. Ferguson's name is visible on the side of the pub in this picture. In 1978 the Greyhound was refurbished for cabaret acts, and in the 1990s went through a series of remodellings as the Cosmic Comedy Club, the Astro Bar and, finally, the Puzzle, with its old interior stripped out and replaced by the inevitable huge, single, pastel-hued space.

The Queen's Head at 13 Brook Green is another early pub, being listed on the 1722 Victuallers' Return, at which time it was called the Maiden Head. The present building was put up in the late nineteenth century and is shown here in 1936, when it was owned by the Isleworth Brewery. It was heavily revamped in the late 1990s and now specialises in food, with a very long menu.

five

Hammersmith

Top: The ornate bar of the old George, Hammersmith Broadway, on the day of its closure, 18 August 1911. The George, despite its slight change of site, is one of the longest surviving pubs in the borough. The George, originally called the White Horse, was subject to an annual charge of 30s left to the poor by Nathaniel Dauncer in his will in 1656.

Above: The entrance to the stables of the old George, Hammersmith Broadway, before 1911 but probably after much of the stabling for this former coaching inn was demolished in 1868. As a booking house for stagecoaches, it originally had extensive stabling and coach houses, which were demolished when the re-sited Metropolitan line terminus was built on the land behind the pub.

Opposite: The Two Georges. In 1911 the old George was closed down and a new larger pub was built behind the old as part of the scheme to widen Hammersmith Broadway. The Royal Sussex Arms to the left of the George was also demolished. The new George was designed by Parr and Kates, and is Grade II listed for its Jacobean-style stone-tiled façade and chimneys.

Hammersmith Broadway, probably in 1924, showing some of the large advertising signs for which the Broadway was once renowned. The Swan is on the left, making much of its 'Afternoon Teas at Popular Prices'. The Metropolitan Line station in the centre of the picture advertises trains to the British Empire Exhibition at White City. The building on the right of the picture was demolished in 1925.

Right: The elegant Swan at Hammersmith Broadway, built in 1901 to a design by F. Miller, replaced an earlier pub which had been a booking house for stagecoaches. The mosaic swan picture at the top of the building is a well-known local landmark. Like the George nearby, the Swan is Grade II listed. Pictured here in September 1978, the Swan is currently called 'Edwards'.

Below: Hammersmith Broadway some time between 1908 and 1910, showing the Royal Sussex Arms and its much less opulent neighbour the George, both of which were to be demolished, along with the early cinema to their right, in 1911 when the Broadway was widened.

Above: The Cannon, Queen Street, in the early twentieth century, showing a large sign for Sich's Entire (i.e. range) of Chiswick Ales, Stout and Porter. Sich's was later absorbed into Fuller Smith and Turner. The Cannon was established in the eighteenth century – the bow window at first-floor level was probably a more recent addition.

Right: The forge at the Plough and Harrow, King Street, 1903, presumably shortly before the old building was demolished to make way for the imposing new hotel.

Below: The old Plough and Harrow, 122 King Street. The name Plough and Harrow on this site allegedly goes back to 1419, and certainly in 1669 Churchwardens' records state 'for the man at the plouge, 02.06'. A new and grander pub was built on the site in 1903; it closed in 1960 and became a car showroom. In 2002 it was demolished, but due to local protest the old façade was kept and installed on the replacement building, which is built slightly further to the right than the old house and has a pub called the Plough and Harrow on its ground floor.

Opposite below: The former Queen Street, running between Hammersmith Broadway and the riverside, is now Queen Caroline Street, named after the estranged wife of George IV. On the list returned by the Hammersmith Law and Parliamentary Committee in 1906 (about the time this picture was taken), seven pubs and beerhouses are named on Queen Street: the Devonshire Arms, the Anchor, the Six Bells, the Duke of Edinburgh, the Hope, the Cannon and the Cabin.

The Hop Poles, 17-19 King Street, on 20 May 1903, decorated for the procession of King Edward VII. The Hop Poles, probably taking its name from the gangs of locals who would provide seasonal labour for the Kentish hopfields, was built in 1857 and is Grade II listed. Although recently renovated (with the same name), it is largely unchanged to the exterior.

The Hop Poles, 17-19 King Street, depicted from the then new King's Mall in 1980.

The Windsor Castle, 134–6 King Street, in 1898. The reason for the huge gathering is uncertain. This pub had a small theatre upstairs in the late eighteenth century, and meeting rooms were hired out to the Methodists in 1806-09. The earliest record of a pub on the site dates from 1753. The current building dates from the late nineteenth century and was extended forwards just before the Second World War.

The Windsor Castle, around 1895. The pub sign is unusually large, though larger signs were in use in the area in the nineteenth century, for example at the Goat (at Hammersmith Broadway), where the sign extended across the street. Above the pub's central window is a sign reading 'Changed to a public house pursuant to the Act of Parliament of the twenty-fifth [year] of King George the Second' (i.e. 1752). This was later replaced by a sign reading WINDSOR CASTLE.

This mid-1970s view of the Builders (otherwise the Builders Arms), 81 King Street, is unusual in that St Paul's Church is visible in the background, the shops to the east of the pub having been demolished and the site cleared for redevelopment. The Builders Arms was built in 1930 and was originally the Angel, but took the name of the old Builders Arms on Bridge Road. It is now called the Hammersmith Ram, and is still a Young's pub.

The Coachmakers Arms, 135-7 King Street, seen in 1918. The reason for the crowd is unknown but may be to welcome soldiers returning from the front. The Electric Palace cinema to the right of the picture (here showing Mary Pickford in *The Beast at Bay*) later became known as the Classic and was finally demolished in 1959. The Coachmakers Arms was built in 1900 and, while largely unchanged externally (the big 'Charrington's Entire' sign at first-floor level is intact), it became a gay pub called the Penny Farthing in the 1980s and in September 2002 reopened as a bar called the Autumn House.

A banquet in session at the Clarendon, Hammersmith Broadway, in the 1950s. As all those present are male it may have some connection with the Masonic lodge which operated upstairs.

A Vanderbilt coach outside the Clarendon. At the western end of Hammersmith Road, the Clarendon replaced earlier pubs called the Goat and the Suspension Bridge. It was named after Edward, Earl of Clarendon (1608-74).

Above: The Carpenter's Arms, Black Lion Lane, pre-1900. Mr Hillier, the landlord, is getting into the gig. As is quite common at the time, the name of the pub is dwarfed by that of the landlord and the advertisements for the beer he sells. The Carpenter's Arms in the St Peter's Square area became a French-themed bar/restaurant called Le St Pierre in 1994.

Left: The Cross Keys, 57 Black Lion Lane, takes its name from the Papal insignia, as it is very close to St Peter's Church. Founded in the early nineteenth century, it is now a Fuller's house. The brickwork on the lower part of the walls seen in this shot from 1974 has unfortunately now been painted over white.

The Raven, 375 Goldhawk Road, in a drawing by Joan Bloxam from the 1920s or 1930s.
The Raven was in existence in 1839 and was originally a stable block. The name is related
to Ravenscourt, the nearby eighteenth-century manor house (bombed in the Second World
War) and the park around it.

The Distiller's Arms, Fulham Palace Road, on 29 May 1980, named after the former
Hammersmith Distillery nearby. In the late 1980s, the Distiller's Arms hosted the 'Wooden
Lambs' live poetry nights after they moved from Chiswick via a temporary home at the
Barons Alehouse. A few years later, the landlord carried out a practical joke on much of the
population of Hammersmith just before he left: he advertised a 'closing down sale' where all
kinds of household and electronic goods were for sale at ten per cent of their list price.
Hundreds of people went to the Distiller's Arms to find the sale didn't exist.

The Dartmouth Castle was founded in 1868 and is the only Glenthorne Road pub still operating under its original name. This picture dates from 25 May 1978 and the pub has not changed much since, though the site to the right of the picture has been built on, depriving the outside area of some of its light.

The Duke of Cornwall, 48 Fulham Palace Road, around 1912. The pub was rebuilt in 1933 and has retained a largely intact 1930s frontage. During the last years of the twentieth century it was an Irish-themed pub called Finnegan's Wake, but has since been refurbished and returned to its earlier name, with the original marbling restored.

The Cock and Magpie, on the north side of King Street, depicted in 1905 in a postcard postmarked '16/8/1910'.

The Hampshire Hog, King Street, on 8 February 1982. By this time the pub had taken over the former shop to the left of the central doorway.

Left: The new Hampshire Hog, built in the late nineteenth century, seen here on 12 May 1973. Since this picture was taken the pub has been extended to occupy the whole lower floor of the building (the whole Hog, so to speak). It is presently known as the Hampshire, and has succumbed to the trend of pubs along King Street resembling bars and nightclubs.

Below: The Ravenscourt Arms, on the south side of King Street at number 243, was a favourite watering-hole of the painter Ruskin Spear. In this picture from October 1957 are the pub, Harry's Snack Bar (with outside seating!), and the archway leading to Thames Place. This pub was demolished and replaced in the 1970s to permit the widening of King Street.

Above: The Hope and Anchor, 20 Macbeth Street, on 19 April 1975. This unpretentious local pub around the back of Hammersmith Town Hall boasts a largely unspoiled two-bar interior and a colonnade at the back. Charles Fletcher was its landlord for sixty years, from 1910 until his death aged eighty-two in 1970, the longest tenancy in London.

Right: The Salutation, 154 King Street, was designed by A.P. Killick and built in 1910, replacing an eighteenth-century house on the site. It is Grade II listed, with particularly fine lustrous faience façade tiling in purple and blue and an entrance hall tiled in cream with a blue dado. The Salutation's sign now depicts Sir Walter Raleigh laying down his cloak for Queen Elizabeth, but the original meaning of the name is religious. There is also a well-maintained back garden.

Above: The very boxy new Ravenscourt Arms in May 1973. The new pub was opened on 12 July 1966, attended by the Mayor, Cllr L.W. Freeman. The current pub is much frequented by people from Waterford, Ireland. Outside the Ravenscourt Arms is the Grade II listed statue of a bull, originally the sign of the Black Bull Inn in Holborn and then acquired by William Bull (MP for Hammersmith, 1900-28).

Left: The White Hart, 383 King Street, appears on the 1722 Magistrates' List and may have seventeenth-century origins; a meeting of Protestant Dissenters took place at the White Hart in 1706. The present building – seen here on 12 May 1973 – was built in 1880. The name was recently shortened to the Hart and the pub has had a makeover as a modern bar.

Right: The programme of Beaconsfield Football Club's Annual Concert, 'at the Richmond Hotel, Shepherd's Bush, W', on Saturday 28 March, 1903, 'Kick-off 8 p.m. sharp'. The programme includes several popular songs of the day, a humourist and conjurer, 'gramophone selections' and a ventriloquist. Item 5, 'Mr Geo Paine (The Beaconsfield Favourite)' has been laconically marked 'Ill'.

Below: Depicted here in May 1974, the Richmond at 55 Shepherd's Bush Road dates from 1869 and is mentioned in the census for 1871 when the licensee was Richard Cosh. The name probably derives from the Richmond and Kensington Railway which followed the paths of the Hammersmith & City and West London railways, with a loop between the two just south of Shepherd's Bush Green. Also opened in 1869, the line closed during the First World War and is now largely built on. The pub was modernised in 1897 and 1947 and the brick cladding added in 1953.

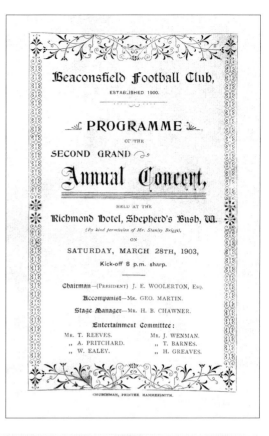

Beaconsfield Football Club,

ESTABLISHED 1900.

❧ PROGRAMME ❧

OF THE

SECOND GRAND

Annual Concert,

HELD AT THE

Richmond Hotel, Shepherd's Bush, W.

(By kind permission of Mr. Stanley Briggs),

ON

SATURDAY, MARCH 28TH, 1903,

Kick-off 8 p.m. sharp.

Chairman—(PRESIDENT) J. E. WOOLERTON, ESQ.

Accompanist—MR. GEO. MARTIN.

Stage Manager—MR. H. B. CHAWNER.

Entertainment Committee:

MR. T. REEVES.	MR. J. WENMAN.
„ A. PRITCHARD.	„ T. BARNES.
„ W. EALEY.	„ H. GREAVES.

CHURCHMAN, PRINTER HAMMERSMITH.

The Andover Arms, 57 Aldensley Road, in the 1970s. This is still a regular 'local' which has not succumbed to the London fashion of gastro-pub makeovers, keeping a good, old-fashioned interior, and is now a Fuller's house. It first appeared in the rate book for 1878, and is in the CAMRA *Good Beer Guide*, 2004.

The Thatched House is in Dalling Road, previously called Albion Road, a short distance north of Hammersmith Broadway. The building is documented to 1793 though the front part with its ornamental balcony may be more recent. Depicted here in the mid-1960s, it is still a Young's pub. The current inn sign depicts swallows and the building does seem to be a magnet for birds, though more usually pigeons.

The Six Bells, 33 Queen Street, on a damp day in November 1929. Around this time Hammersmith and Fulham reached its all-time peak population of 288,000; it has little more than half that nowadays.

The Duke of Edinburgh, 52a Queen Caroline Street, on the corner of Worlidge Street, in the 1960s. This was rebuilt in 1898 (note the sign at the top of the building) and demolished when the area was cleared post-war and the Queen Caroline estate was built.

The Britannia, Fulham Palace Road, some time in 1896-97. The Electors List for 1896 gives 'Holmes, Walter, 17 Fulham Palace Road' and 'Stephens, Charles Henry, 19 Fulham Palace Road'. The 1895 and 1898 lists give no C.H. Stephens, so his bicycle shop may have been very short-lived.

The Brook Green Hotel, Shepherd's Bush Road, on a windy day in the late nineteenth century.

The Britannia, Hammersmith Broadway, some time just after the Second World War. The old Britannia, rebuilt in 1906, was demolished in 1957 to make way for the Hammersmith flyover. Charles Faulkener, then ninety-four years old, said in August 1976, 'It [the old pub] was old and dirty. It was a good thing they pulled it down.'

The Brook Green Hotel, Shepherd's Bush Road, on 24 January 1975, with a number 9 bus outside it. The road scheme has been changed since the buildings behind the hotel were demolished, and the number 9 bus route no longer passes it.

Above: The Red Cow, 157 Hammersmith Road, depicted in 1892. It appears on the 1722 Victuallers' Return and in 1768 was put up for sale as the Cow Alehouse. To its left, on the corner of Cow Lane (now Colet Gardens), was a horse dealer's yard, relevant in the days of coaching when the Red Cow was one end of the route from London to Bath. Here, the *Daily Graphic* for 21 September 1896 tells us, 'the Crown coach changed its elegant horses from the Belle Sauvage for the sturdier animals for Bath and Bristol'. The satirical painter Rowlandson painted a picture with the Red Cow in the background; Dr Burney, father of Fanny Burney, the author of *Evelina*, ran a school nearby from 1786 to 1793. In 1896-97, as the *Graphic*'s article lamented, the picturesque old Red Cow was demolished. Its replacement, bearing the same name, was a three-storey hotel with a curious lantern dome.

Opposite above: The staff of the Cannon, probably in the 1950s. Unfortunately no names have been recorded for this picture.

Opposite below: The Cambridge Arms, Cambridge Grove, on 9 April 1973. The Cambridge Arms, now called the Stonemason's Arms, is on the corner of Glenthorne Road, which at one time had three more pubs – the Eagle Arms, the Royal Oak, and the Dartmouth Castle. Only the last now survives as a pub. The Stonemason's Arms, in common with many pub rebuilds, knocked the two bars of the original pub into one, but the exterior is unaltered, keeping the original sash windows and a fine plaster coat of arms at first-floor level.

The Prince of Wales, an Irish pub in Dalling Road, pictured some time in the 1950s or 1960s. In 1879 it was described as a 'house of call' for the Amalgamated Society of Engineers, Machinists, Millwrights, Smiths and Pattern Makers. In 2002 it was turned into an Irish-themed pub called Tommy Flynn's.

The Red Cow – seen here on 14 May 1973 – became first of all a Country and Western pub and then a venue for aspiring Punk bands, hosting Elvis Costello, AC/DC and the Stranglers among others. The pub was also used during the making of the TV series *The Sweeney*; the crews used it during the filming and some scenes took place there. The Red Cow closed to live music at the end of August 1978 and closed down at the end of that year. It was demolished in 1981 and a new office block, incorporating a pub, was built on the site. The pub was opened in 1988 as the Red Cow and renamed Latymer's in 1989.

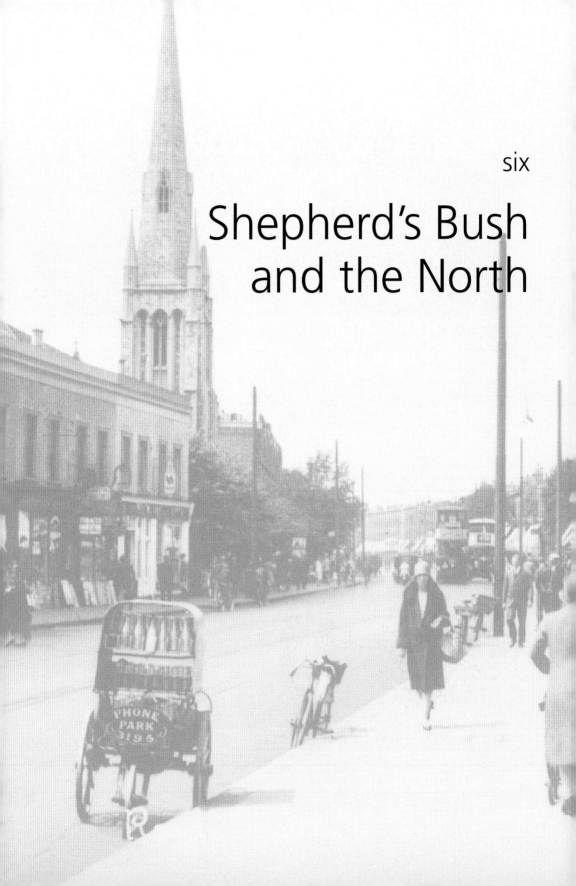

six

Shepherd's Bush
and the North

The College Park Hotel at 873 Harrow Road, almost the northernmost point of the borough. The College Park closed down in the mid-1990s and has now been renovated and converted to housing. The huge 'Double Diamond' sign in the picture, which was taken on 17 May 1976, covers a plaster shield saying 'College Park Hotel', which is now the only sign of its former identity. The area was land previously owned by an Abbey and at the dissolution was passed to All Souls' College, Oxford, hence the name.

The North Pole, at the corner of North Pole Road and Latimer Road, 19 May 1977. When this picture was taken it was a Watneys tavern advertising live music. There are now few pubs in the northern part of the borough: the Oak Tree, at the corner of Western Avenue and Old Oak Common Lane, burned down on 21 June 1985, and was replaced by a homecare store. The North Pole is still functioning.

The new Duke of Sussex, on the corner of Queensdale Crescent and St Anne's Road W11, on 28 May 1977. This pub is now renamed the Favourite.

The old Duke of Sussex in Poynter Street W11, now long gone. The street layout around the area between St Anne's Road and the railway has been much changed due to the building of the Edward Woods housing estate, which is under Hammersmith and Fulham borough jurisdiction (although generally land to the east of the railway is the Royal Borough of Kensington and Chelsea).

Left: A group outside the Stewart Arms, Norland Road, around 1910. The family to the left are probably those of the landlord, T. Luff, whose name appears over the door. The Stewart Arms is still in operation though is now in the Borough of Kensington and Chelsea.

Below: The General Smuts, Bloemfontein Road (White City), on 13 September 1977. The Smuts was originally proposed in 1938 when a Watneys house was removed to make way for flats. The house was finally opened in September 1952 at a cost of £67,000. The name, which is now controversial, was chosen because of imperial connections in the road names of the neighbourhood; the Greyhound and the Hare had also been suggested.

Opposite below: The Coningham Arms, Uxbridge Road, on 1 March 1976. Founded in 1881, it is still in use. Like the Princess Victoria (q.v.) and the British Queen on the other side of the road, it is much frequented by Irish supporters of Celtic FC.

Above: The Askew Arms, 269 Uxbridge Road, on 1 March 1976. At the time it was an Ind Coope pub, here seen advertising Double Diamond. The Askew Arms was built around 1900 and is externally largely unchanged from the picture, except that the name has been abbreviated to the Askew.

Above: The Greyhound, Becklow Road, on 19 May 1975. Built in the 1880s, the Greyhound shows well-preserved stucco features and a slate roof. It is still in use as a small Irish local for the area.

Left: The Orchard Tavern, 136 Askew Road, on 12 June 1975. The Orchard, dating from the 1880s, is an unpretentious establishment serving the local Irish community.

Right: The Goldhawk Hotel at 122 Goldhawk Road, showing for some reason a drawn-on dimension of the large sign outside, on 24 January 1928. The Goldhawk was built in 1858 and its outside appearance is still much the same, while the interior has been converted into one large space and given an up-to-date look with wooden floors, leather sofas and low-level lighting.

Below: The Eagle, Askew Road, on 12 June 1975. Although the main house dates from the late nineteenth century, the small lean-to on the left of the entrance is much earlier, being half of a structure which appears on a J. Chalmers painting from 1857. The Eagle, which is still extant, was originally called the Lady of the Lake, a very uncommon name.

The old Mail Coach, 28 Uxbridge Road, on the north side of Shepherd's Bush Green. There was an inn on this site from at least 1839 when mail coaches would stop here, the easternmost end of the Uxbridge Road.

The Moon on the Green, now known simply as the Green, was opened in a previously unused end-of-terrace block at 172 Uxbridge Road some time in the late 1980s, directly opposite the Beaumont Arms (now Edward's) and facing the north-western corner of Shepherd's Bush Green. This picture was taken on 14 April 1993.

The Pavilion, Pavilion Parade, Wood Lane, in 1977. Originally called the Rifle Pavilion, it was built to serve the rifle range on Wormwood Scrubs which was set up in the 1850s when the Hammersmith Volunteers were founded. It later became the Pavilion Hotel. The site of the rifle range is now occupied by the West London Stadium.

Founded in 1829 on the corner of Victoria Road (now Becklow Road) and rebuilt in 1880, the Princess Victoria is one of several large pubs serving the Uxbridge Road, for many years the main thoroughfare westwards, and serves as a local focus for Celtic FC supporters. The hotel-like and ornate Princess Victoria is here depicted in May 1975, when it was a Watneys house.

Above: The Railway Tavern, 55 Goldhawk Road, on 12 June 1975. Like the Railway Arms across the road (p.121), it was built in the late nineteenth century to capitalise on the railway trade from what was then a Shepherd's Bush station sited where Shepherd's Bush market is now. In 1914 that station was replaced by Goldhawk Road station, even closer to this pub. In 1976 the Railway Tavern was renamed the Bushranger, to display its link with Queen's Park Rangers FC and its location in Shepherd's Bush. In 1982 it was heavily revamped, but without losing its pub atmosphere.

Opposite above: The Springbok, South Africa Road, on 13 September 1977. This pub is near Queen's Park Rangers' Loftus Road ground and is popular with supporters. During the mid-1980s it was known as McQueen's but reverted to its original name by the early 1990s.

Opposite below: The Wellington Arms, Uxbridge Road, on the north side of Shepherd's Bush Green, around 1900. The pub workers are dealing with a large number of barrels outside; this may be delivery day or getting rid of the empties.

Above: The Wellington Arms, also around 1900. Dick Blanchard was the licensee from 1892-93 to 1903-04. The Wellington was rebuilt in 1905. It is now the Slug and Lettuce, aimed at the youth market as most pubs around the borough's town centres are.

Above: The Wheatsheaf, formerly the Dukes and now the Brackenbury Arms, a small Irish pub at 163 Goldhawk Road. Built in the mid-nineteenth century and possessing some interesting ironwork above the entrance, it is shown here in 1965.

Opposite: The Sun, Askew Road, is one of the longest-established pubs in the borough, being named on a list from 1716. Here, in its incarnation as a tiled Victorian building, it is depicted some time in the 1930s. This inn was destroyed in an air raid on 25 September 1940, and a new establishment opened in 1960.

Above: The White Horse, 31 Uxbridge Road, depicted in 1976. In recent years this pub has been divided so that only the right-hand bay of the original house remains, the rest having been converted into a shop. This results in an odd-shaped premises where the entrance area is narrower than the rest of the pub.

Right: The Bush Hotel, 2 Goldhawk Road, on 8 September 1973. Built in 1890 on the site of the old Brewery Tavern and originally called the White Horse, it was renamed the Bush in 1899 to avoid confusion with the White Horse in Uxbridge Road. It later became the Fringe and Firkin and is now an O'Neill's bar.

Below: The saloon bar of the White Horse in Uxbridge Road, 1910 with a woman, presumably the landlady, using the ornate Edwardian till.

Opposite below: Uxbridge Road in the 1920s, with a collection of carriages and bicycles, and the White Horse pub on the left. The White Horse was built in the 1850s. In the wall there is a milestone reading: 'Uxbridge XII miles Marble Arch III miles'.

The Beaumont Arms, 170 Uxbridge Road, after an air raid on the night of 6 November 1940, in which two were killed and four injured. Worse was to befall other pubs in the area and their inhabitants: the Telegraph (Richmond Road) was hit on 26 October 1940, killing twenty people.

The remains of the Sun, Askew Road, after the air raid of 25 September 1940, when it was bombed just before closing time, with major loss of life. Strangely, Perton's Builders' Supply Store to the left is all but untouched.

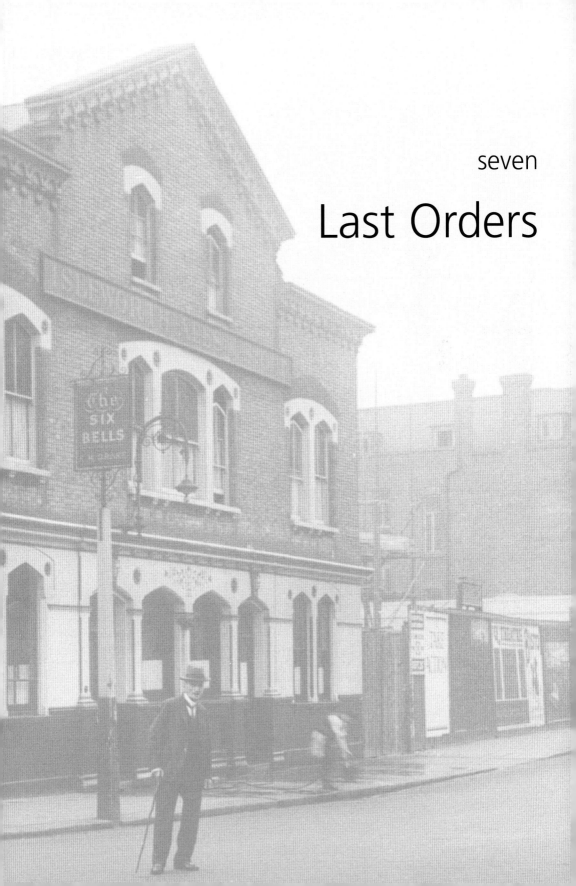

seven

Last Orders

Above: The Ship, on the corner of (Hammersmith) Bridge Road and Ship Lane, very close to the Thames, in 1909. It has now gone, being replaced by the Queen Caroline estate, nor is there any sign of Ship Lane. The Old Ship was given the prefix 'Old' to distinguish it from this pub.

Left: The White Bear, at 100 King Street, a pub that appears on the 1722 register. In 1747 a man, probably a tailor, 'dressed in a blue coat, scarlet waistcoat and breeches', took lodging there and hanged himself in the night. This picture dates from around 1900, and the pub was in business until 1910 or later, although by the time of the picture it was a smaller house than before. This reduced building survives and is in use as a pizza restaurant.

Opposite below: The Windsor Castle, 134–136 King Street, in 1905. The man and woman to the right of the picture are probably the landlord and landlady. To the left someone obviously didn't realise his picture was being taken. The pub was closed in the 1960s, converted by Tesco into a supermarket, and is now two shops.

Above: The Cock and Magpie, 170 King Street, depicted around 1910. The Cock and Magpie was an eighteenth-century pub that survived alongside much newer buildings. The site is now occupied by an office block called Thanet House, 170 King Street.

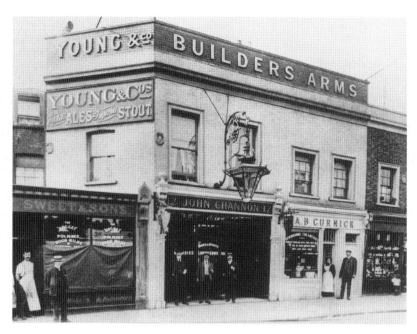

The old Builders Arms on (Hammersmith) Bridge Road in the late nineteenth century. In 1894 there were five pubs on Bridge Road; only two (the Old City Arms and the Oxford and Cambridge) survive. The Builders Arms was demolished in the 1950s, and the name transferred to the former Angel in King Street.

The sign over the door of the Maltman and Shovel, pictured in 1964. The Maltman and Shovel was at 6 King Street, next door to the present-day William Morris, and was named after the malthouses which were landmarks on the riverside and up Hammersmith Creek. In the Hammersmith Street Directory of 1863 it is ascribed to 'Philpott G., licensed victuallers'. During the construction of the William Morris in 1997-98, the cellar of the Maltman and Shovel was apparently uncovered, with bottles still remaining in it.

The Hope in Beavor Lane, at the edge of the St Peter's Square area, in the 1930s. This was one of three pubs serving the area: the others were the Cross Keys (still there) and the Carpenter's Arms (now a French-themed café and restaurant). The Hope is now an office block.

The Eagle Arms, 82-84 Glenthorne Road, shortly after it closed down. This pub appears on the 1906 official list as the Eagle. By the time this picture was taken in 1998, the façade including the tiling on the lower part had been painted over in dark pink. This building still stands and is in use as offices, but in 2003 there was an application to demolish.

By the 1940s, four of Queen Caroline Street's old pubs were still in existence: the Devonshire Arms, the Six Bells (see opposite below), the Duke of Edinburgh (see p.120), and the Cannon (pictured here 6 May 1936). In the 1970s the last of these was swept away in favour of modern housing.

The Queen of England on the corner of Goldhawk Road and Stamford Brook Road, on 12 June 1975. For a time Charlotte's Wine Bar and Brooks, this is now a restaurant called the Café Med.

For much of the twentieth century the Clarendon, Hammersmith Broadway, was a fashionable place to have dinner or cocktails: this is the American or Cocktail bar. Later on it became a music venue, and finally succumbed to the redevelopment of central Hammersmith in the late 1980s. The ornamental glass from the windows was salvaged by an American collector who went on to become a stained-glass maker.

The Six Bells at the top of Queen Caroline Street, pictured on 3 October 1931. Originating in the eighteenth century, it was rebuilt in the late nineteenth century. By the late 1950s it stood alone, a short distance in front of the Gaumont (now the Hammersmith Apollo), and was demolished in 1959 to make way for the A4 flyover.

Above: The Californian, 1-2 St Thomas Way, in 1957. Nothing now remains of this pub, which had been the Duke of Edinburgh in 1890 and 1901. In the intervening years it was not always a pub: in electoral lists for 1953 it is shown as a bookshop.

Right: The Railway Arms, on the north side of Goldhawk Road by Goldhawk Road underground station, in 1975. Confusingly, it was just opposite the Railway Tavern. It was completely rebuilt in 1992 and is now a fabric and furnishings shop.

Below: The Norfolk Arms, 272 North End Road, on 24 January 1974. Built in 1894, it served North End Road market for many decades until it closed some time after 1979. The structure is now used as a building society branch.

Opposite below: The Lord Clyde at 124 Estcourt Road, a short way south of Lillie Road, was extended in 1889 due to increased business 'since the occupancy of Mr C. Elgie'. It was rated at £150 in 1890 with a proposed increase to £200. Pictured here on a winter afternoon in 1957, the Lord Clyde was demolished in 1971 and replaced by the Clem Attlee (now the Pump House). The Clem Attlee housing estate is visible in the left background of the picture. Estcourt Road now terminates at Rylston Road instead of crossing it as it did before the Clem Attlee was built. Opposite the Lord Clyde was the Redan, which is now a tyre shop.

The Three Jolly Gardeners,
215-7 Hammersmith
Road, on 21 May 1972.
This, like the Rose and
Crown at 203
Hammersmith Road, was
demolished shortly after
this shot was taken. The
picture echoes a drawing
made by A.O. Collard in
1910 and, apart from the
modern block to the left of
the photograph is largely
identical. Parts of the
Three Jolly Gardeners were
probably seventeenth-
century or even earlier,
containing panelled
Georgian rooms and an
original beam roof.

The Rose and Crown,
203 Hammersmith Road,
pictured by the
Hammersmith and Fulham
Local History librarian,
Christine Bayliss, on
21 May 1972. The ornate
Rose and Crown was
demolished shortly after
this picture was taken to
make way for the widening
of Hammersmith Road.
Along with the pub, the
Rowton House directly
behind it (one of six hostels
for homeless working men
built around London in the
late nineteenth century)
and the Latymer Lower
School were lost at this
time, as well as two more
pubs, the Jolly Gardeners at
no.217 and the Wheatsheaf
at no.241.

The Sheepshank, 7 Swanscombe Road W11, just north of Holland Park Avenue, in July 1981. This modern building served as an estate pub for the Edward Woods estate, but was demolished in recent years. It is now a derelict site awaiting redevelopment.

The Victoria, 61 Latimer Road at the corner of Hunt Street, in 1965. This pub, and Hunt Street itself, were pulled down to make room for the Westway (A40) and West Cross Route. There is now a Hunt Street on the Edward Woods estate but it is not the same place. The building of the new roads also put an end to Norland Road with its market and its two pubs, the Royal Hotel and the Queen's Arms.

Above: A totter's cart negotiates hazardous motor traffic near the Trafalgar, 2 Bramley Road, in the 1960s. This pub would have been opposite the Bramley Arms (q.v.) but is no longer in existence, being replaced by an office block.

Right: The elegant Bramley Arms was an end-of-terrace pub on the borders of North Kensington. Unfortunately, it has long since closed down and is now used for small office space. It is shown here on 28 May 1977.

Below: The new Britannia (seen here in September 1978), once described as 'like an estate pub without the estate', was a box-like structure on the other side of the road from its predecessor. Although it advertised its 'beer garden' it was rather too close to the A4 traffic for comfortable sitting outside. The Britannia was demolished in 1988 as part of the Broadway redevelopment project.

Opposite below: The Royal Oak, Glenthorne Road, on 9 August 1970. A Royal Oak is mentioned in the 1722 Victuallers' List, and is likely to have been a precursor of this house. The probably twentieth-century building seen here flourished as a pub until the late 1990s, being a gay pub with drag cabaret in its last incarnation, but is now a table-dancing club.

Left: The Princess Alexandra, 1 Perrers Road, in the Brackenbury area of Hammersmith, in September 1973. In 1984 it was an early gastro-pub, run by the Jeffs family and offering Dover sole for £5.50, grilled rib of pork for £2, and 40g of Beluga caviar for £60! It may have been ahead of its time, for it has long since closed down, like the Duke of York opposite it, and is now a private house.

Below: The new Mail Coach, designed by W. Blomfield and built in 1932 after purchase by Goodhews Ltd. This picture dates from June 1973 and shows the arch and halls of the White City complex, built in 1908 for Imre Kiralfy's Franco-British Exhibition. The White City buildings and the arch, as well as the Mail Coach, were demolished in 2003 to make way for the Chelsfield retail/residential development. At the time of its demolition it was a cosy Irish pub with London Underground memorabilia on the walls.

Worth a Visit

Despite all the changes of recent years which have seen traditional pub interiors stripped out and replaced by an increasingly homogenous style of décor, a number stand out as largely unspoilt and worth a visit if you are in the area, or even coming from further afield.

W6 (Hammersmith)

The Andover Arms, 57 Aldensley Road
The Blue Anchor, 13 Lower Mall
The Black Lion, 2 Black Lion Lane South
The Brook Green, 170 Shepherd's Bush Road
The Dove, 19 Upper Mall
The Hope and Anchor, Riverside Gardens
The Queen's Head, 13 Brook Green
The Raven, 375 Goldhawk Road

W12 (Shepherd's Bush)

The Greyhound, 49 Becklow Road

W14 (Brook Green and North Fulham)

The Colton Arms, 187 Greyhound Road
The Old Parr's Head, 120 Blythe Road
The Seven Stars, 253 North End Road
The Queen's Arms, 171 Greyhound Road

SW6 (Fulham)

The Atlas, 16 Seagrave Road
The Duke of Cumberland, 235 New King's Road
The Eight Bells, 89 Fulham High Street
The Golden Lion, 57 Fulham High Street
The White Hart, 563 Fulham Road
The White Horse, 1-3 Parsons Green

Other local titles published by Tempus

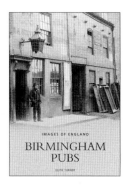

Birmingham Pubs
KEITH TURNER

A century ago there were more than 1,500 hotels, inns, taverns and public houses in Birmingham. Using more than 200 photographs and other illustrations from the late 1850s to the early 1970s, this book forms an evocative record of some of them and includes examples that survive – and many more that have gone for ever. *Birmingham Pubs* is a unique record of an important part of Birmingham's social history.
7524 1809 2

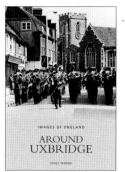

Around Uxbridge
JAMES SKINNER

Compiled with over 220 archive photographs, this fascinating volume provides a glimpse into the history of Uxbridge during the last century, capturing images of sport and recreation, education and religion, public servces and family firms, events and personalities, as well as the local people who have lived and worked in and around Uxbridge.
7524 3205 2

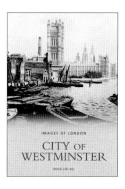

City of Westminster
BRIAN GIRLING

This collection of old photgraphs of one of Britain's best known areas recalls the Edwardian period of London's old City of Westminster. Using over 200 images this volume leads the reader around Pimlico through Belgravia and Knightsbridge, Mayfair and St James' and on to Soho and the West End's famous theatreland. *City of Westminster* will appeal to all who know Westminster whether as home, a place of work or as a place to visit.
7524 3191 9

Wolverhampton Pubs
ALEC BREW

This comprehensive volume of archive images recalls the history, popularity and changing role of any of Wolverhampton's pubs, from the First World War through to the present day. Illustrated with over 200 old photographs and postcards, this collection recalls local characters and lively landlords. It also charts the changing façades of the town's pubs, from street corner pubs to the imposing new pubs built between the wars.
7524 3156 0

If you are interested in purchasing other books published by Tempus, or in case you have difficulty finding any Tempus books in your local bookshop, you can also place orders directly through our website
www.tempus-publishing.com